Description:

_____

_____

_____

_____

_____

_____

_____

_____

_____

_____

_____

_____

Sky Placement:

Time:

_____

Weather:

_____

Lunar Phase:

_____

Longitude:

_____

Latitude:

_____

Objects Sited:

_____

_____

_____

_____

Equipment Used:

_____

Additional Notes:

Date: ____/____/____

_____

_____

_____

_____

_____

_____

_____

_____

_____

_____

_____

_____

_____

Sketches & Photos:

Description: Date: ____/____/____

_____

_____

_____

_____

_____

_____

_____

_____

_____

_____

_____

_____

Place:

_____

_____

Time:

_____

Weather:

_____

Lunar Phase:

_____

Longitude:

_____

Latitude:

_____

Objects Sited:

_____

_____

_____

_____

Equipment Used:

_____

Sky Placement:

3

Additional Notes: Date: ____/____/____

_____
_____
_____
_____
_____
_____
_____
_____
_____
_____
_____
_____
_____
_____

Sketches & Photos:

Description:

Date: ____/____/____

_____

_____

_____

_____

_____

_____

_____

_____

_____

_____

_____

_____

_____

_____

Sky Placement:

Place:

_____

_____

Time:

_____

Weather:

_____

Lunar Phase:

_____

Longitude:

_____

Latitude:

_____

Objects Sited:

_____

_____

_____

_____

Equipment Used:

_____

5

Additional Notes:

Date: ____/____/____

_____

_____

_____

_____

_____

_____

_____

_____

_____

_____

_____

_____

_____

Sketches & Photos:

Description:

Date: ____/____/____

_____

_____

_____

_____

_____

_____

_____

_____

_____

_____

_____

_____

_____

Place:

_____

_____

Time:

_____

Weather:

_____

Lunar Phase:

_____

Longitude:

_____

Latitude:

_____

Objects Sited:

_____

_____

_____

_____

Equipment Used:

_____

Sky Placement:

7

Additional Notes:

Date: ____/____/____

_____

_____

_____

_____

_____

_____

_____

_____

_____

_____

_____

_____

Sketches & Photos:

Description:

_____
_____
_____
_____
_____
_____
_____
_____
_____
_____
_____
_____
_____
_____

Sky Placement:

Date: ____/____/____

Place:
_____

_____

Time:
_____

Weather:
_____

Lunar Phase:
_____

Longitude:
_____

Latitude:
_____

Objects Sited:
_____

_____

_____

_____

Equipment Used:
_____

Additional Notes:

Date: ____/____/____

_____

_____

_____

_____

_____

_____

_____

_____

_____

_____

_____

Sketches & Photos:

Description:

Date: ____/____/____

_____

_____

_____

_____

_____

_____

_____

_____

_____

_____

_____

_____

Sky Placement:

Place:

_____

_____

Time:

_____

Weather:

_____

Lunar Phase:

_____

Longitude:

_____

Latitude:

_____

Objects Sited:

_____

_____

_____

_____

Equipment Used:

_____

11

Additional Notes:

_____

_____

_____

_____

_____

_____

_____

_____

_____

_____

_____

_____

Sketches & Photos:

Description:

_____
_____
_____
_____
_____
_____
_____
_____
_____
_____
_____
_____

Date: ____/____/____

Place:

_____

Time:

_____

Weather:

_____

Lunar Phase:

_____

Longitude:

_____

Latitude:

_____

Objects Sited:

_____
_____
_____
_____

Equipment Used:

_____

Sky Placement:

Additional Notes:

_____

_____

_____

_____

_____

_____

_____

_____

_____

_____

_____

_____

Sketches & Photos:

Description:

Date: ____/____/____

_____

_____

_____

_____

_____

_____

_____

_____

_____

_____

_____

_____

_____

_____

Sky Placement:

Place:

_____

_____

Time:

_____

Weather:

_____

Lunar Phase:

_____

Longitude:

_____

Latitude:

_____

Objects Sited:

_____

_____

_____

_____

Equipment Used:

_____

15

Additional Notes:

_____

_____

_____

_____

_____

_____

_____

_____

_____

_____

_____

_____

Sketches & Photos:

Description:

_____

_____

_____

_____

_____

_____

_____

_____

_____

_____

_____

_____

Sky Placement:

Date: ____/____/____

Place:

_____

_____

Time:

_____

Weather:

_____

Lunar Phase:

_____

Longitude:

_____

Latitude:

_____

Objects Sited:

_____

_____

_____

_____

Equipment Used:

_____

Additional Notes:

Date: ____/____/____

_____
_____
_____
_____
_____
_____
_____
_____
_____
_____
_____
_____

Sketches & Photos:

Description:

Date: ____/____/____

_____

_____

_____

_____

_____

_____

_____

_____

_____

_____

_____

_____

Sky Placement:

Place:

_____

_____

Time:

_____

Weather:

_____

Lunar Phase:

_____

Longitude:

_____

Latitude:

_____

Objects Sited:

_____

_____

_____

_____

Equipment Used:

_____

19

Additional Notes:

_____

_____

_____

_____

_____

_____

_____

_____

_____

_____

_____

_____

Sketches & Photos:

Description:

Date: ____/____/____

_____

_____

_____

_____

_____

_____

_____

_____

_____

_____

_____

_____

_____

Place:

_____

_____

Time:

_____

Weather:

_____

Lunar Phase:

_____

Longitude:

_____

Latitude:

_____

Objects Sited:

_____

_____

_____

_____

Sky Placement:

Equipment Used:

_____

21

Additional Notes:

Sketches & Photos:

Description:

Date: ____/____/____

_____

_____

_____

_____

_____

_____

_____

_____

_____

_____

_____

_____

Sky Placement:

Place:

_____

_____

Time:

_____

Weather:

_____

Lunar Phase:

_____

Longitude:

_____

Latitude:

_____

Objects Sited:

_____

_____

_____

_____

Equipment Used:

_____

Additional Notes:

Date: ____/____/____

_____
_____
_____
_____
_____
_____
_____
_____
_____
_____
_____
_____
_____

Sketches & Photos:

Description:

Date: ____/____/____

_____
_____
_____
_____
_____
_____
_____
_____
_____
_____
_____
_____

Place:
_____
_____

Time:
_____

Weather:
_____

Lunar Phase:
_____

Longitude:
_____

Latitude:
_____

Objects Sited:
_____
_____
_____
_____

Equipment Used:
_____

Sky Placement:

Additional Notes:

Sketches & Photos:

Description: Date: ___/___/___

_____   Place:
_____
_____   _____
_____
_____   _____
_____
_____   Time:
_____
_____   _____
_____
_____   Weather:
_____
_____   _____
_____
_____   Lunar Phase:
_____
                                     _____

                                     Longitude:

                                     _____

Sky Placement: Latitude:

                                     _____

                                     Objects Sited:

                                     _____

                                     _____

                                     _____

                                     _____

                                     Equipment Used:

                                     _____

27

Additional Notes:

Date: ___/___/___

_____

_____

_____

_____

_____

_____

_____

_____

_____

_____

_____

_____

Sketches & Photos:

Description:

_____

_____

_____

_____

_____

_____

_____

_____

_____

_____

_____

_____

_____

_____

Sky Placement:

Date: ____/____/____

Place:

_____

_____

Time:

_____

Weather:

_____

Lunar Phase:

_____

Longitude:

_____

Latitude:

_____

Objects Sited:

_____

_____

_____

_____

Equipment Used:

_____

Additional Notes: Date: ____/____/____

_____
_____
_____
_____
_____
_____
_____
_____
_____
_____
_____
_____

Sketches & Photos:

Description:

_____
_____
_____
_____
_____
_____
_____
_____
_____
_____
_____

Sky Placement:

Date: ____/____/____

Place:

_____

Time:

_____

Weather:

_____

Lunar Phase:

_____

Longitude:

_____

Latitude:

_____

Objects Sited:

_____
_____
_____
_____

Equipment Used:

_____

Additional Notes:

_____

_____

_____

_____

_____

_____

_____

_____

_____

_____

_____

_____

Sketches & Photos:

Description:

Date: ____/____/____

_____

_____

_____

_____

_____

_____

_____

_____

_____

_____

_____

_____

Place:

_____

_____

Time:

_____

Weather:

_____

Lunar Phase:

_____

Longitude:

_____

Latitude:

_____

Objects Sited:

_____

_____

_____

_____

Equipment Used:

_____

Sky Placement:

Additional Notes:

_____

_____

_____

_____

_____

_____

_____

_____

_____

_____

_____

_____

Sketches & Photos:

Description:

Date: ____/____/____

_____

Place:

_____

_____

_____

_____

_____

Time:

_____

_____

_____

Weather:

_____

_____

_____

Lunar Phase:

_____

_____

_____

Longitude:

_____

_____

Sky Placement:

Latitude:

_____

Objects Sited:

_____

_____

_____

_____

Equipment Used:

_____

Additional Notes:

Sketches & Photos:

Description:

Date: ____/____/____

_____

_____

_____

_____

_____

_____

_____

_____

_____

_____

_____

_____

Place:

_____

_____

Time:

_____

Weather:

_____

Lunar Phase:

_____

Longitude:

_____

Latitude:

_____

Objects Sited:

_____

_____

_____

_____

Equipment Used:

_____

Sky Placement:

37

Additional Notes:

Date: ____/____/____

Sketches & Photos:

Description:

Date: ____/____/____

_____

_____

_____

_____

_____

_____

_____

_____

_____

_____

_____

_____

Place:

_____

_____

Time:

_____

Weather:

_____

Lunar Phase:

_____

Longitude:

_____

Sky Placement:

Latitude:

_____

Objects Sited:

_____

_____

_____

_____

Equipment Used:

_____

Additional Notes: Date: ____/____/____

_____

_____

_____

_____

_____

_____

_____

_____

_____

_____

_____

_____

Sketches & Photos:

Description:

Date: ____/____/____

_____

_____

_____

_____

_____

_____

_____

_____

_____

_____

_____

_____

Place:

_____

_____

Time:

_____

Weather:

_____

Lunar Phase:

_____

Longitude:

_____

Latitude:

_____

Objects Sited:

_____

_____

_____

_____

Equipment Used:

_____

Sky Placement:

Additional Notes:

_____

_____

_____

_____

_____

_____

_____

_____

_____

_____

_____

Sketches & Photos:

Description:

Date: ___/___/___

_____

_____

_____

_____

_____

_____

_____

_____

_____

_____

_____

_____

Place:

_____

_____

Time:

_____

Weather:

_____

Lunar Phase:

_____

Longitude:

_____

Latitude:

_____

Objects Sited:

_____

_____

_____

_____

Equipment Used:

_____

Sky Placement:

Additional Notes:

Date: ____/____/____

_____

_____

_____

_____

_____

_____

_____

_____

_____

_____

_____

_____

Sketches & Photos:

Description:

Date: ____/____/____

_____

_____

_____

_____

_____

_____

_____

_____

_____

_____

_____

_____

Place:

_____

_____

Time:

_____

Weather:

_____

Lunar Phase:

_____

Longitude:

_____

Latitude:

_____

Objects Sited:

_____

_____

_____

_____

Equipment Used:

_____

Sky Placement:

Additional Notes: Date: ____/____/____

_____

_____

_____

_____

_____

_____

_____

_____

_____

_____

_____

_____

Sketches & Photos:

Description:

Date: ___/___/___

Place:
_____
_____

Time:
_____

Weather:
_____

Lunar Phase:
_____

Longitude:
_____

Sky Placement:

Latitude:
_____

Objects Sited:
_____
_____
_____
_____

Equipment Used:
_____

Additional Notes:

Date: ____/____/____

_____

_____

_____

_____

_____

_____

_____

_____

_____

_____

_____

_____

Sketches & Photos:

Description:

Date: ____/____/____

_____
_____
_____
_____
_____
_____
_____
_____
_____
_____
_____
_____

Place:

_____

_____

Time:

_____

Weather:

_____

Lunar Phase:

_____

Longitude:

_____

Latitude:

_____

Objects Sited:

_____

_____

_____

_____

Equipment Used:

_____

Sky Placement:

49

Additional Notes:

Date: ____/____/____

Sketches & Photos:

Description:

Date: ___/___/___

_____

_____

_____

_____

_____

_____

_____

_____

_____

_____

_____

Sky Placement:

Place:

_____

_____

Time:

_____

Weather:

_____

Lunar Phase:

_____

Longitude:

_____

Latitude:

_____

Objects Sited:

_____

_____

_____

_____

Equipment Used:

_____

Additional Notes: Date: ____/____/____

_____
_____
_____
_____
_____
_____
_____
_____
_____
_____
_____
_____
_____

Sketches & Photos:

Description:

Date: ____/____/____

_____

_____

_____

_____

_____

_____

_____

_____

_____

_____

_____

_____

Place:

_____

_____

Time:

_____

Weather:

_____

Lunar Phase:

_____

Longitude:

_____

Latitude:

_____

Objects Sited:

_____

_____

_____

_____

Equipment Used:

_____

Sky Placement:

Additional Notes:

Date: _____/_____/_____

_____

_____

_____

_____

_____

_____

_____

_____

_____

_____

_____

_____

Sketches & Photos:

Description:

_____
_____
_____
_____
_____
_____
_____
_____
_____
_____
_____
_____

Sky Placement:

Date: ____/____/____

Place:

_____

_____

Time:

_____

Weather:

_____

Lunar Phase:

_____

Longitude:

_____

Latitude:

_____

Objects Sited:

_____

_____

_____

_____

Equipment Used:

_____

55

Additional Notes:

_____

_____

_____

_____

_____

_____

_____

_____

_____

_____

_____

_____

Sketches & Photos:

Description:

Date: ____/____/____

_____

_____

_____

_____

_____

_____

_____

_____

_____

_____

_____

_____

Sky Placement:

Place:

_____

_____

Time:

_____

Weather:

_____

Lunar Phase:

_____

Longitude:

_____

Latitude:

_____

Objects Sited:

_____

_____

_____

Equipment Used:

_____

Additional Notes: Date: ____/____/___

_____
_____
_____
_____
_____
_____
_____
_____
_____
_____
_____
_____
_____
_____
_____

Sketches & Photos:

Description:

Date: ____/____/____

_____

_____

_____

_____

_____

_____

_____

_____

_____

_____

_____

_____

Place:

_____

_____

Time:

_____

Weather:

_____

Lunar Phase:

_____

Longitude:

_____

Latitude:

_____

Objects Sited:

_____

_____

_____

_____

Equipment Used:

_____

Sky Placement:

Additional Notes:

_____

_____

_____

_____

_____

_____

_____

_____

_____

_____

_____

_____

Sketches & Photos:

Description:

Date: ____/____/____

_____

_____

_____

_____

_____

_____

_____

_____

_____

_____

_____

_____

Sky Placement:

Place:

_____

_____

Time:

_____

Weather:

_____

Lunar Phase:

_____

Longitude:

_____

Latitude:

_____

Objects Sited:

_____

_____

_____

_____

Equipment Used:

_____

61

Additional Notes:

_____

_____

_____

_____

_____

_____

_____

_____

_____

_____

_____

_____

Sketches & Photos:

Description:

Date: ____/____/____

_____

_____

_____

_____

_____

_____

_____

_____

_____

_____

_____

_____

_____

Sky Placement:

Place:

_____

_____

Time:

_____

Weather:

_____

Lunar Phase:

_____

Longitude:

_____

Latitude:

_____

Objects Sited:

_____

_____

_____

_____

Equipment Used:

_____

Additional Notes:

Date: _____/_____/_____

_____
_____
_____
_____
_____
_____
_____
_____
_____
_____
_____
_____
_____
_____

Sketches & Photos:

Description:

Date: ___/___/___

_____

_____

_____

_____

_____

_____

_____

_____

_____

_____

_____

_____

_____

Sky Placement:

Place:

_____

_____

Time:

_____

Weather:

_____

Lunar Phase:

_____

Longitude:

_____

Latitude:

_____

Objects Sited:

_____

_____

_____

_____

Equipment Used:

_____

Additional Notes:

_____

_____

_____

_____

_____

_____

_____

_____

_____

_____

_____

_____

Sketches & Photos:

Description:

Date: ____/____/____

_____

_____

_____

_____

_____

_____

_____

_____

_____

_____

_____

_____

Place:

_____

_____

Time:

_____

Weather:

_____

Lunar Phase:

_____

Longitude:

_____

Latitude:

_____

Objects Sited:

_____

_____

_____

_____

Sky Placement:

Equipment Used:

_____

Additional Notes: Date: ____/____/____

_____

_____

_____

_____

_____

_____

_____

_____

_____

_____

_____

_____

Sketches & Photos:

Description:

Date: ____/____/____

_____

_____

_____

_____

_____

_____

_____

_____

_____

_____

_____

_____

_____

Sky Placement:

Place:

_____

_____

Time:

_____

Weather:

_____

Lunar Phase:

_____

Longitude:

_____

Latitude:

_____

Objects Sited:

_____

_____

_____

_____

Equipment Used:

_____

Additional Notes:

Date: ____/____/____

Sketches & Photos:

Description:

Date: ___/___/___

_____

_____

_____

_____

_____

_____

_____

_____

_____

_____

_____

_____

_____

Sky Placement:

Place:

_____

_____

Time:

_____

Weather:

_____

Lunar Phase:

_____

Longitude:

_____

Latitude:

_____

Objects Sited:

_____

_____

_____

_____

Equipment Used:

_____

Additional Notes:

Date: _____/_____/_____

_____

_____

_____

_____

_____

_____

_____

_____

_____

_____

_____

_____

Sketches & Photos:

Description:

Date: ____/____/____

_____

_____

_____

_____

_____

_____

_____

_____

_____

_____

_____

_____

_____

Place:

_____

_____

Time:

_____

Weather:

_____

Lunar Phase:

_____

Longitude:

_____

Latitude:

_____

Objects Sited:

_____

_____

_____

_____

Equipment Used:

_____

Sky Placement:

73

Additional Notes: Date: ____/____/____

_____
_____
_____
_____
_____
_____
_____
_____
_____
_____
_____
_____
_____

Sketches & Photos:

Description:

Date: ____/____/____

_____

Place:

_____

_____

Time:

Weather:

Lunar Phase:

Longitude:

Sky Placement:

Latitude:

Objects Sited:

Equipment Used:

75

Additional Notes: Date: ____/____/____

_____
_____
_____
_____
_____
_____
_____
_____
_____
_____
_____
_____
_____

Sketches & Photos:

Description:

Date: ___/___/___

_____

_____

_____

_____

_____

_____

_____

_____

_____

_____

_____

Place:

_____

_____

Time:

_____

Weather:

_____

Lunar Phase:

_____

Longitude:

_____

Latitude:

_____

Objects Sited:

_____

_____

_____

_____

Equipment Used:

_____

Sky Placement:

Additional Notes: Date: ____/____/____

_____

_____

_____

_____

_____

_____

_____

_____

_____

_____

_____

_____

Sketches & Photos:

Description:

Date: ____/____/____

_____

_____

_____

_____

_____

_____

_____

_____

_____

_____

_____

_____

Place:

_____

_____

Time:

_____

Weather:

_____

Lunar Phase:

_____

Longitude:

_____

Latitude:

_____

Objects Sited:

_____

_____

_____

_____

Equipment Used:

_____

Sky Placement:

Additional Notes: Date: ____/____/____

_____

_____

_____

_____

_____

_____

_____

_____

_____

_____

_____

_____

Sketches & Photos:

Description:

Date: ____/____/____

_____

_____

_____

_____

_____

_____

_____

_____

_____

_____

_____

_____

Place:

_____

_____

Time:

_____

Weather:

_____

Lunar Phase:

_____

Longitude:

_____

Latitude:

_____

Objects Sited:

_____

_____

_____

_____

Equipment Used:

_____

Sky Placement:

Additional Notes: Date: ___/___/___

_____

_____

_____

_____

_____

_____

_____

_____

_____

_____

_____

Sketches & Photos:

Description:

Date: ____/____/____

_____
_____
_____
_____
_____
_____
_____
_____
_____
_____
_____

Place:

_____

_____

Time:

_____

Weather:

_____

Lunar Phase:

_____

Longitude:

_____

Latitude:

_____

Objects Sited:

_____

_____

_____

_____

Equipment Used:

_____

Sky Placement:

83

Additional Notes: Date: ____/____/____

_____

_____

_____

_____

_____

_____

_____

_____

_____

_____

_____

_____

Sketches & Photos:

Description: Date: ____/____/____

_____

_____

_____

_____

_____

_____

_____

_____

_____

_____

_____

Sky Placement:

Place:

_____

_____

Time:

_____

Weather:

_____

Lunar Phase:

_____

Longitude:

_____

Latitude:

_____

Objects Sited:

_____

_____

_____

_____

Equipment Used:

_____

85

Additional Notes:

Date: ____/____/____

Sketches & Photos:

Description:

Date: ____/____/____

_____

_____

_____

_____

_____

_____

_____

_____

_____

_____

_____

_____

Place:

_____

_____

Time:

_____

Weather:

_____

Lunar Phase:

_____

Longitude:

_____

Latitude:

_____

Objects Sited:

_____

_____

_____

_____

Equipment Used:

_____

Sky Placement:

Additional Notes: Date: ____/____/____

_____
_____
_____
_____
_____
_____
_____
_____
_____
_____
_____
_____

Sketches & Photos:

Description: Date: ___/___/___

_____   Place:
_____
_____   _____
_____   _____
_____
_____   Time:
_____
_____   _____
_____
_____   Weather:
_____
_____   _____
_____
_____   Lunar Phase:
_____
_____   _____

                                Longitude:

                                _____

Sky Placement: Latitude:

                                _____

                                Objects Sited:

                                _____
                                _____
                                _____
                                _____

                                Equipment Used:

                                _____

Additional Notes: Date: ____/____/____

_____
_____
_____
_____
_____
_____
_____
_____
_____
_____
_____
_____

Sketches & Photos:

Description:

Date: ___/___/___

Place:
_____
_____

Time:
_____

Weather:
_____

Lunar Phase:
_____

Longitude:
_____

Sky Placement:

Latitude:
_____

Objects Sited:
_____
_____
_____
_____

Equipment Used:
_____

Additional Notes:

_____

_____

_____

_____

_____

_____

_____

_____

_____

_____

_____

_____

Sketches & Photos:

Description:

Date: ___/___/___

_____

_____

_____

_____

_____

_____

_____

_____

_____

_____

_____

_____

Sky Placement:

Place:

_____

_____

Time:

_____

Weather:

_____

Lunar Phase:

_____

Longitude:

_____

Latitude:

_____

Objects Sited:

_____

_____

_____

_____

Equipment Used:

_____

Additional Notes: Date: ____/____/____

_____
_____
_____
_____
_____
_____
_____
_____
_____
_____
_____
_____

Sketches & Photos:

Description: Date: ___/___/___

_____   Place:

_____   _____

_____   _____

_____   Time:

_____   _____

_____   Weather:

_____   _____

_____   Lunar Phase:

_____   _____

_____   Longitude:

_____   _____

Sky Placement: Latitude:

                                        _____

                                        Objects Sited:

                                        _____

                                        _____

                                        _____

                                        _____

                                        Equipment Used:

                                        _____

Additional Notes:

Date: _____/_____/_____

_____
_____
_____
_____
_____
_____
_____
_____
_____
_____
_____
_____
_____
_____

Sketches & Photos:

Description:

Date: ____/____/____

_____

_____

_____

_____

_____

_____

_____

_____

_____

_____

_____

_____

_____

Sky Placement:

Place:

_____

_____

Time:

_____

Weather:

_____

Lunar Phase:

_____

Longitude:

_____

Latitude:

_____

Objects Sited:

_____

_____

_____

_____

Equipment Used:

_____

Additional Notes:

Date: ____/____/____

_____

_____

_____

_____

_____

_____

_____

_____

_____

_____

_____

_____

_____

Sketches & Photos:

Description:

Date: ___/___/___

_____

_____

_____

_____

_____

_____

_____

_____

_____

_____

_____

_____

Place:

_____

_____

Time:

_____

Weather:

_____

Lunar Phase:

_____

Longitude:

_____

Latitude:

_____

Objects Sited:

_____

_____

_____

_____

Equipment Used:

_____

Sky Placement:

Additional Notes:

Date: ___/___/___

Sketches & Photos:

Description:

Date: ____/____/____

_____

_____

_____

_____

_____

_____

_____

_____

_____

_____

_____

_____

Place:

_____

_____

Time:

_____

Weather:

_____

Lunar Phase:

_____

Longitude:

_____

Latitude:

_____

Objects Sited:

_____

_____

_____

_____

Equipment Used:

_____

Sky Placement:

Additional Notes: Date: ____/____/____

_____
_____
_____
_____
_____
_____
_____
_____
_____
_____
_____
_____
_____

Sketches & Photos:

Description:

Date: ____/____/____

_____

_____

_____

_____

_____

_____

_____

_____

_____

_____

_____

_____

_____

Place:

_____

_____

Time:

_____

Weather:

_____

Lunar Phase:

_____

Longitude:

_____

Latitude:

_____

Objects Sited:

_____

_____

_____

_____

Equipment Used:

_____

Sky Placement:

Additional Notes:

Sketches & Photos:

Description:

Date: ____/____/____

_____

_____

_____

_____

_____

_____

_____

_____

_____

_____

_____

Sky Placement:

Place:

_____

_____

Time:

_____

Weather:

_____

Lunar Phase:

_____

Longitude:

_____

Latitude:

_____

Objects Sited:

_____

_____

_____

_____

Equipment Used:

_____

Additional Notes: Date: ____/____/____

_____
_____
_____
_____
_____
_____
_____
_____
_____
_____
_____
_____
_____

Sketches & Photos:

Description:

Date: ___/___/___

_____

_____

_____

_____

_____

_____

_____

_____

_____

_____

_____

_____

_____

Place:

_____

_____

Time:

_____

Weather:

_____

Lunar Phase:

_____

Longitude:

_____

Latitude:

_____

Objects Sited:

_____

_____

_____

_____

Equipment Used:

_____

Sky Placement:

Additional Notes: Date: ____/____/____

_____

_____

_____

_____

_____

_____

_____

_____

_____

_____

_____

_____

Sketches & Photos:

Printed in Great Britain
by Amazon

49558581R00066